The Ultimate Emeril Lagasse French Door Large Air Fryer Oven Cookbook

1500 Days of Mouthwatering Recipes to Transform Any Meal, Ideal for Gatherings, Showcasing Regular Sides, Bites, Sweet Treats & Beyond| Full Color Edition

Wendy C. Thomas

Manufactured in: USA

Cover Art: DANIELLE REES

Interior Design: DANIELLE REES

Art Producer: BROOKE WHITE

Production Editor: SIENNA ADAMS

Editor: AALIYAH LYONS

Production Manager: SARAH JOHNSON

Photography: MICHAEL SMITH

Table Of Contents

Introduction   1

Chapter 1
Introducing Your Emeril Air Fryer Oven   2
Exploring the Cooking Functions   3
Tips for Perfectly Air-Fried Foods   4
Frequently Asked Questions   5
Air Fryer Cooking Chart   6

Chapter 2
Breakfast Recipes   8
Hash Brown Egg Cups   9
Creamy Sausage and Cauliflower   9
Baked Breakfast Oatmeal   10

Sweet Potato Breakfast Bake   10
Breakfast Pizzas with Muffins   11
Speedy Coffee Donuts   11
Oat and Chia Seeds Porridge   12
Moist Banana Bread   12
Bacon and Ham Cups   13
Savory French Toast   13
Ham and Cheese Scones   14
French Toast Casserole   15

Chapter 3
Snacks and Appetizer Recipes   16
Cheesy Broccoli Bites   17
Cheesy Sweet Onion Dip   17

Spicy Spinach Chips 18
Eggplant Fries 18
Crispy Avocado Fries 19
Whole Artichoke Hearts 20
Nutella Banana Pastries 20
Puffed Egg Tarts 21
Mini Hot Dogs 22
Cajun Dill Pickle Chips 22
Baked Zucchini Tots 23
Crispy Green Olives 23

Chapter 4
Poultry Recipes 24
Chicken Potato Bake 25
Chicken Casserole 25
Spanish Chicken Bake 26
Italian Chicken Breast 26
Cheesy Chicken Cutlets 27
Golden Chicken Nuggets 27
Chicken Wings with Hot Sauce 28
Chicken Breast Pita Sandwich 29
Herbed Duck Breast 30
Lemony Whole Chicken 31

Chapter 5
Beef, Pork and Lamb Recipes 32
Garlicky Lamb Steaks 33
Tarragon Beef Shanks 34
Herbed Chuck Roast 34
Tasty Chicken Drumsticks 35
Greek Lamb Rib Rack 35
Chimichurri Flank Steak 36
Lamb Kebabs 36
Beef Spring Rolls 37
Savory Pork Roast 37
Marinated Steak Bites 38
Roasted Lamb Leg 38
Rosemary Beef Roast 39
Double Cheese Beef Meatballs 39

Chapter 6
Fish and Seafood Recipes 40
Garlic Butter Salmon Bites 41
Herbed Shrimp 41

Bacon-Wrapped Scallops with Salad 42
Lime Blackened Shrimp Tacos 43
Prawns in Butter Sauce 44
New Orleans Crab Cakes 44

Chapter 7 45
Vegetables and Sides Recipes 45
Herbed Bell Peppers 46
Beans & Veggie Burgers 46
Sweet & Spicy Parsnips 47
Tomato Zucchini Bake 47
Sweet & Tangy Mushrooms 48
Asparagus with Garlic and Parmesan 48
Smoky Wax Beans 49
Rosemary Green Beans 49
Wine Braised Mushrooms 50

Chapter 8
Dessert Recipes 51
Scalloped Pineapple 52
Choco Chip Bars 52
Bourbon Vanilla Bread Pudding 53
Roasted Cashews 53
Roasted Honey Pears 54
Banana and Nuts Cake 54
Creamy Lime Mousse 55
Peanut Brittle Bars 55

Chapter 9
Dehydrated and Rotisserie Recipes 56
Mushroom Slices 57
Nutritious Almonds 57
Dried Pineapple Pieces 58
Pork Jerky 58
Zucchini Chips 60
Prime Rib Roast with Mustard Rub 61

Appendix 1 Measurement Conversion Chart 62
Appendix 2 The Dirty Dozen and Clean Fifteen 63
Appendix 3 Index 64

Introduction

Last year, on my birthday, I received a remarkable gift from my husband, David. As I unwrapped the box, my eyes widened in surprise and delight at the sight of an Emeril Lagasse French Door Large Air Fryer Oven. David knows I love experimenting in the kitchen, but this gift took my culinary adventures to a whole new level.

From the moment I plugged it in, that air fryer oven became my kitchen companion, and it didn't take long for it to become my favorite appliance. Its sleek design and versatility inspired me to create dishes I never thought possible. With just a few button presses, I could roast, bake, toast, and air fry with precision and ease.

The convenience of the French door design made accessing my creations a breeze, and soon enough, my kitchen was filled with the aroma of delicious meals made in the easiest way possible. From crispy fries to succulent chicken, the Emeril Lagasse air fryer oven transformed my cooking experience, allowing me to whip up gourmet meals with minimal time and effort.

Dedication

To David, just wanted to give you a big shoutout for not only hooking me up with that awesome Emeril Lagasse Air Fryer Oven but for also being my partner in cooking adventures! It's been a blast researching recipes and whipping up delicious meals together after work and on weekends. Your enthusiasm and support mean the world to me, and it's made our culinary journey even more enjoyable. Here's to many more tasty dishes and memorable moments shared together.

Chapter 1

Introducing Your Emeril Air Fryer Oven

Exploring the Cooking Functions

Ready to dive into the world of delicious possibilities with your Emeril Air Fryer Oven? Awesome, let's get started! Today, we're going to take a closer look at the fantastic cooking functions packed into this bad boy. Get ready to unleash your inner chef and create culinary masterpieces like never before.

AIR FRY

Let's kick things off with a fan favorite – the air fry function. Say goodbye to greasy, unhealthy fried foods and hello to crispy goodness without the guilt. This function uses superheated air to give your dishes that perfect golden-brown crunch. From fries to chicken wings, you'll be amazed at how crispy and delicious your favorites turn out.

BAKE

Who needs a traditional oven when you've got the bake function on your Emeril Air Fryer Oven? Whether you're whipping up a batch of cookies or baking a homemade pizza, this function has got you covered. With precise temperature control and even heat distribution, you can achieve bakery-quality results right in your own kitchen.

TOAST

Say goodbye to burnt toast forever! The toast function on your air fryer oven ensures perfectly toasted bread every time. Whether you prefer a light golden hue or a crispy crunch, you can customize the level of toastiness to suit your taste. Plus, with the spacious interior of the French door design, you can toast multiple slices at once – perfect for feeding a hungry crowd.

BROIL

Need to quickly sear a steak or melt cheese on top of your favorite dish? The broil function has got your back. With high, direct heat, you can achieve that mouthwatering caramelization and crispy exterior without overcooking the inside. It's perfect for adding that extra touch of flavor and texture to your meals.

ROAST

Get ready to roast like a pro with the roast function. Whether you're cooking up a succulent chicken or a tender roast beef, this function locks in flavor and moisture for mouthwatering results every time. Plus, with the large capacity of your air fryer oven, you can roast whole vegetables alongside your main dish for a complete meal with minimal effort.

DEHYDRATE

Want to make your own homemade dried fruit or jerky? The dehydrate function makes it easy. Simply set the temperature and time, and let your air fryer oven do the rest. Say goodbye to store-bought snacks packed with preservatives – with the dehydrate function, you can enjoy healthy, homemade treats whenever you want.

REHEAT

Tired of soggy leftovers? The reheat function is here to save the day. Whether you're warming up last night's dinner or reheating a slice of pizza, this function ensures even heating without drying out your food. Say hello to leftovers that taste just as good as they did the first time around.

Tips for Perfectly Air-Fried Foods

Alright, let's talk about the secret sauce to achieving crispy, golden perfection with your air fryer. Whether you're whipping up fries, chicken wings, or veggies, these tips will take your air-fried creations to the next level. So grab your apron and let's get frying!

- Preheat Like a Pro: Just like with a traditional oven, preheating your air fryer is key to getting that crispy exterior. Most air fryers have a preheat function, so be sure to give it a few minutes to heat up before adding your food. This helps ensure even cooking and that perfect crunch we all love.
- Don't Overcrowd: It can be tempting to fill up your air fryer basket to the brim, but resist the urge! Overcrowding can lead to uneven cooking and soggy results. Instead, give your food some room to breathe. Spread it out in a single layer, making sure there's space between each piece for the hot air to circulate.
- Oil It Up: While one of the perks of air frying is using less oil than traditional frying methods, a little bit goes a long way in achieving that crispy texture. Before adding your food to the basket, lightly coat it with a thin layer of oil. This helps promote browning and gives your dishes that irresistible crunch.
- Shake, Shake, Shake: To ensure even cooking and crispy results, give your basket a shake halfway through the cooking time. This helps redistribute the food and prevents any pieces from sticking together. Plus, it's a great excuse to show off your culinary skills with a little kitchen dance!
- Check for Doneness: Unlike traditional frying, you can't rely on the color of your food to determine if it's done in the air fryer. Instead, use a meat thermometer to check the internal temperature of meats and seafood. For veggies and other foods, give them a quick poke with a fork to check for tenderness. Remember, practice makes perfect – soon you'll be able to nail the timing without even thinking about it.
- Get Creative with Seasonings: One of the best things about air frying is how versatile it is. Don't be afraid to experiment with different seasonings and flavor combinations to take your dishes to the next level. Whether you're craving classic salt and pepper or something more adventurous like Cajun seasoning or garlic herb blend, the sky's the limit!
- Let It Rest: Just like with any other cooking method, it's important to let your air-fried goodies rest for a few minutes before digging in. This allows the flavors to meld together and ensures that perfect crispy texture. Plus, it gives you a chance to snap a quick pic for the 'gram before you devour them!
- Clean Up with Ease: After you've satisfied your cravings, cleaning up your air fryer is a breeze. Most models have dishwasher-safe baskets and trays, making cleanup a snap. If you prefer to hand wash, simply soak the parts in warm, soapy water for a few minutes before giving them a quick scrub. Voila – good as new and ready for your next culinary adventure!

Frequently Asked Questions

HOW DOES AN AIR FRYER WORK?

Think of an air fryer as a mini convection oven on steroids. It uses hot air circulated at high speed to cook food, creating that crispy exterior we all love without the need for a ton of oil. It's like magic for your taste buds!

IS AIR FRYING HEALTHIER THAN TRADITIONAL FRYING?

Absolutely! Air frying typically uses 70-80% less oil than traditional frying methods, making it a healthier alternative. Plus, you still get that delicious crispy texture without all the grease. It's a win-win for your taste buds and your waistline.

WHAT CAN I COOK IN AN AIR FRYER?

The better question is: what can't you cook in an air fryer? From fries and chicken wings to veggies and even desserts, the possibilities are endless. Get creative and experiment with your favorite recipes – you might be surprised at what you can whip up!

DO I NEED TO PREHEAT MY AIR FRYER?

While preheating isn't always necessary, it can help ensure more even cooking and crispier results. Most air fryers have a preheat function, so give it a few minutes to heat up before adding your food for best results.

CAN I USE ALUMINUM FOIL OR PARCH-MENT PAPER IN MY AIR FRYER?

Absolutely! Aluminum foil and parchment paper can both be used in your air fryer to help prevent sticking and make cleanup easier. Just be sure to leave some space around the edges to allow for proper air circulation and avoid covering the entire basket or tray.

WHY IS MY FOOD NOT GETTING CRISPY?

There could be a few reasons why your food isn't getting crispy. Make sure you're not overcrowding the basket, as this can prevent proper air circulation. You may also need to adjust the cooking time or temperature to achieve that perfect crunch. And don't forget to give your basket a shake halfway through cooking to ensure even browning.

CAN I COOK FROZEN FOODS IN MY AIR FRYER?

Absolutely! One of the best things about air frying is its ability to cook frozen foods quickly and evenly. Whether you're craving crispy frozen fries or chicken nuggets, your air fryer can handle it with ease. Just be sure to adjust the cooking time and temperature as needed based on the manufacturer's instructions.

IS IT SAFE TO LEAVE MY AIR FRYER UNATTENDED?

While it's generally safe to leave your air fryer unattended for short periods, it's always a good idea to keep an eye on it, especially if you're cooking something for the first time. Make sure the appliance is placed on a stable, heat-resistant surface away from any flammable materials, and never leave it running overnight or while you're out of the house.

Air Fryer Cooking Chart

Beef					
Item	Temp (°F)	Time (mins)	Item	Temp (°F)	Time (mins)
Beef Eye Round Roast (4 lbs.)	400 °F	45 to 55	Meatballs (1-inch)	370 °F	7
Burger Patty (4 oz.)	370 °F	16 to 20	Meatballs (3-inch)	380 °F	10
Filet Mignon (8 oz.)	400 °F	18	Ribeye, bone-in (1-inch, 8 oz)	400 °F	10 to 15
Flank Steak (1.5 lbs.)	400 °F	12	Sirloin steaks (1-inch, 12 oz)	400 °F	9 to 14
Flank Steak (2 lbs.)	400 °F	20 to 28			

Chicken					
Item	Temp (°F)	Time (mins)	Item	Temp (°F)	Time (mins)
Breasts, bone in (1 1/4 lb.)	370 °F	25	Legs, bone-in lb.)	380 °F	30
Breasts, boneless (4 oz)	380 °F	12	Thighs, boneless (1 1/2 lb.)	380 °F	18 to 20
Drumsticks (2 1/2 lb.)	370 °F	20	Wings (2 lb.)	400 °F	12
Game Hen (halved 2 lb.)	390 °F	20	Whole Chicken	360 °F	75
Thighs, bone-in (2 lb.)	380 °F	22	Tenders	360 °F	8 to 10

Pork & Lamb					
Item	Temp (°F)	Time (mins)	Item	Temp (°F)	Time (mins)
Bacon (regular)	400 °F	5 to 7	Pork Tenderloin	370 °F	15
Bacon (thick cut)	400 °F	6 to 10	Sausages	380 °F	15
Pork Loin (2 lb.)	360 °F	55	Lamb Loin Chops (1-inch thick)	400 °F	8 to 12
Pork Chops, bone in (1-inch, 6.5 oz)	400 °F	12	Rack of Lamb (1.5 - lb.)	380 °F	22
Flank Steak (2 lbs.)	400 °F	20 to 28			

Fish & Seafood					
Item	Temp (°F)	Time (mins)	Item	Temp (°F)	Time (mins)
Calamari (8 oz)	400 °F	4	Tuna Steak	400 °F	7 to 10
Fish Fillet (1-inch, 8 oz)	400 °F	10	Scallops	400 °F	5 to 7
Salmon, fillet (6 oz)	380 °F	12	Shrimp	400 °F	5
Swordfish steak	400 °F	10	Sirloin steaks (1-inch, 12 oz)	400 °F	9 to 14
Flank Steak (2 lbs.)	400 °F	20 to 28			

Vegetables					
INGREDIENT	AMOUNT	PREPARATION	OIL	TEMP	COOK TIME
Asparagus	2 bunches	Cut in half, trim stems	2 Tbsp	420°F	12-15 mins
Beets	1 1/2 lbs	Peel, cut in 1/2-inch cubes	1Tbsp	390°F	28-30 mins
Bell peppers (for roasting)	4 peppers	Cut in quarters, remove seeds	1Tbsp	400°F	15-20 mins
Broccoli	1 large head	Cut in 1-2-inch florets	1Tbsp	400°F	15-20 mins
Brussels sprouts	1lb	Cut in half, remove stems	1Tbsp	425°F	15-20 mins
Carrots	1lb	Peel, cut in 1/4-inch rounds	1 Tbsp	425°F	10-15 mins
Cauliflower	1 head	Cut in 1-2-inch florets	2 Tbsp	400°F	20-22 mins
Corn on the cob	7 ears	Whole ears, remove husks	1 Tbps	400°F	14-17 mins
Green beans	1 bag (12 oz)	Trim	1 Tbps	420°F	18-20 mins
Kale (for chips)	4 OZ	Tear into pieces, remove stems	None	325°F	5-8 mins
Mushrooms	16 OZ	Rinse, slice thinly	1 Tbps	390°F	25-30 mins
Potatoes, russet	11/2 lbs	Cut in 1-inch wedges	1 Tbps	390°F	25-30 mins
Potatoes, russet	1lb	Hand-cut fries, soak 30 mins in cold water, then pat dry	1/2 -3 Tbps	400°F	25-28 mins
Potatoes, sweet	1lb	Hand-cut fries, soak 30 mins in cold water, then pat dry	1 Tbps	400°F	25-28 mins
Zucchini	1lb	Cut in eighths lengthwise, then cut in half	1 Tbps	400°F	15-20 mins

Chapter 2

Breakfast Recipes

Hash Brown Egg Cups

Prep time: 5 minutes | Cook time: 30 minutes |Serves 12

- 8 eggs
- 2 tbsp milk
- 1/4 tsp garlic powder
- 1 cup ham, cubed
- 1 1/2 cups cheddar cheese, grated
- 20 oz hash browns
- Pepper
- Salt

1. Spray 12-cups muffin pan with cooking spray and set aside.
2. In a bowl, whisk eggs with milk, pepper, and salt. Add ham, cheese, and hash browns and stir to combine.
3. Pour egg mixture into the greased muffin pan.
4. Select bake then set the temperature to 350°F and time to 30 minutes. Press start.
5. Once the oven is preheated then place the muffin pan into the oven.
6. Serve and enjoy.

Creamy Sausage and Cauliflower

Prep time: 5 minutes | Cook time: 45 minutes | Serves 4

- 1 pound sausage, cooked and crumbled
- 2 cups heavy whipping cream
- 1 head cauliflower, chopped
- 1 cup grated Cheddar cheese, plus more for topping
- 8 eggs, beaten
- Salt and ground black pepper, to taste

1. Select the BAKE function and preheat AIR FRYER OVEN to 350°F.
2. In a large bowl, mix the sausage, heavy whipping cream, chopped cauliflower, cheese and eggs. Sprinkle with salt and ground black pepper.
3. Pour the mixture into a greased casserole dish. Bake in the preheated air fryer oven for 45 minutes or until firm.
4. Top with more Cheddar cheese and serve.

Baked Breakfast Oatmeal

Prep time: 5 minutes | Cook time: 30 minutes |Serves 8

- 2 eggs
- 3 cups rolled oats
- 1/4 cup butter, melted
- 1/2 cup maple syrup
- 1 1/2 cups almond milk
- 1 tsp ground cinnamon
- 1 tsp vanilla
- 1 1/2 tsp baking powder
- Pinch of salt

1. Place rack in the bottom position and close door. Select bake mode set the temperature to 350°F and set the timer to 30 minutes. Press the setting dial to preheat.
2. In a bowl, whisk eggs with milk, cinnamon, butter, vanilla, baking powder, maple syrup, and salt.
3. Add oats and mix well.
4. Pour the mixture into the greased baking pan.
5. Once the unit is preheated, open the door, and place the baking pan onto the center of the rack, and close the door.
6. Serve and enjoy.

Sweet Potato Breakfast Bake

Prep time: 5 minutes | Cook time: 60 minutes |Serves 8

- 3 eggs
- 3/4 tsp cinnamon
- 1/4 cup coconut flour
- 1/4 cup raisins
- 1 mashed banana
- 1/3 cup maple syrup
- 2 sweet potatoes, peel & grated
- 1/4 tsp salt

1. In a large bowl, add mashed banana, eggs, maple syrup, raisins, and sweet potatoes and mix well.
2. Add cinnamon, coconut flour, and salt and mix until well combined.
3. Pour mixture into the greased baking dish.
4. Select bake mode then set the temperature to 350°F and time for 60 minutes. Press start.
5. Once the oven is preheated then place the baking dish into the oven.
6. Slice and serve.

Breakfast Pizzas with Muffins

Prep Time: 5 minutes |Cook Time: 6 minutes |Serves 3

- 6 eggs, cooked and scrambled
- 1 pound ground sausage
- ½ cup Colby jack cheese, shredded
- 3 egg muffins, sliced in half
- Olive oil spray

1. Using olive oil cooking spray, spray the air fry basket.
2. Place each half in the basket.
3. Using a light layer of olive oil spray, lightly coat the English muffins and top with scrambled eggs and fried sausages.
4. Add cheese on top of each one.
5. Insert a wire rack on Level 3. Turn on your Air fryer oven and select "Bake".
6. Select the timer for 5 minutes and the temperature for 355 °F.
7. When the unit beeps to show that it has preheated, open the oven and insert the air fry basket on the wire rack of Level 3 in oven.
8. Serve hot.

Speedy Coffee Donuts

Prep time: 5 minutes | Cook time: 6 minutes | Serves 6

- ¼ cup sugar
- ½ tsp salt
- 1 cup flour
- 1 tsp baking powder
- ¼ cup coffee
- 1 tbsp aquafaba
- 1 tbsp sunflower oil

1. In a large bowl, combine the sugar, salt, flour, and baking powder.
2. Add the coffee, aquafaba, and sunflower oil and mix until a dough is formed. Leave the dough to rest in and the refrigerator.
3. Remove the dough from the fridge and divide up, kneading each section into a doughnut.
4. Put the doughnuts inside the air fryer oven. Select the AIR FRY function and cook at 400°F for 6 minutes.
5. Serve immediately.

Oat and Chia Seeds Porridge

Prep time: 10 minutes | Cook time: 5 minutes | Serves 4

- 2 tbsp peanut butter
- 4 tbsp honey
- 1 tbsp butter, melted
- 4 cups milk
- 2 cups oats
- 1 cup chia seeds

1. Select the BAKE function and preheat AIR FRYER OVEN to 390°F.
2. Put the peanut butter, honey, butter, and milk in a bowl and stir to mix. Add the oats and chia seeds and stir.
3. Transfer the mixture to a bowl and bake in the air fryer oven for 5 minutes. Give another stir before serving.

Moist Banana Bread

Prep time: 5 minutes | Cook time: 55 minutes |Serves 12

- 2 eggs
- 3 ripe bananas
- 2 cups flour
- 1/4 tsp cinnamon
- 1 tsp baking soda
- 1 cup sugar
- 1 tsp vanilla
- 1 stick butter, melted
- 1/2 tsp salt

1. Place rack in the bottom position and close door. Select bake mode set the temperature to 350°F and set the timer to 55 minutes. Press the setting dial to preheat.
2. Add bananas and butter to a mixing bowl and mash using a fork.
3. Add eggs and vanilla and stir until well combined.
4. In a separate bowl, mix together flour, baking soda, sugar, cinnamon, and salt,
5. Add flour mixture to the banana mixture and mix until just combined.
6. Pour batter into the greased loaf pan.
7. Once the unit is preheated, open the door, and place the loaf pan onto the center of the rack, and close the door.
8. Slice and serve.

Bacon and Ham Cups

Prep time: 5 minutes | Cook time: 20 minutes | Serves 2

- 3 slices bacon, cooked, sliced in half
- 2 slices ham
- 1 slice tomato
- 2 eggs
- 2 tsp grated Parmesan cheese
- Salt and ground black pepper, to taste

1. Select the BAKE function and preheat AIR FRYER OVEN to 375°F. Line 2 greased muffin tins with 3 half-strips of bacon
2. Put one slice of ham and half slice of tomato in each muffin tin on top of the bacon
3. Crack one egg on top of the tomato in each muffin tin and sprinkle each with half a tsp of grated Parmesan cheese. Sprinkle with salt and ground black pepper, if desired.
4. Bake in the preheated air fryer oven for 20 minutes. Remove from the air fryer oven and let cool.
5. Serve warm.

Savory French Toast

Prep time: 5 minutes | Cook time: 5 minutes | Serves 2

- ¼ cup chickpea flour
- 3 tbsp onion, finely chopped
- 2 tsp green chili, seeded and finely chopped
- ½ tsp red chili powder
- ¼ tsp ground turmeric
- ¼ tsp ground cumin
- Salt, to taste
- Water, as needed
- 4 bread slices

1. Add all the ingredients except bread slices in a large bowl and mix until a thick mixture form.
2. With a spoon, spread the mixture over both sides of each bread slice.
3. Arrange the bread slices into the lightly greased SearPlate.
4. Press AIR OVEN MODE button of Air Fry Oven and turn the dial to select "Air Fry" mode.
5. Press TIME/SLICES button and again turn the dial to set the cooking time to 5 minutes.
6. Now push TEMP/SHADE button and rotate the dial to set the temperature at 390 °F.
7. Press "Start/Stop" button to start.
8. When the unit beeps to show that it is preheated, open the oven door and insert the SearPlate in oven.
9. Flip the bread slices once halfway through.
10. When cooking time is completed, open the oven door and serve warm.

Ham and Cheese Scones

Prep Time: 15 minutes|Cook Time: 25 minutes|Serves 6

- 2 cups all-purpose flour
- 1 tbsp baking powder
- 2 tsp sugar
- 1 tsp kosher salt
- 2 tbsp butter, cubed
- 1 cup ham, diced, cooked
- ¼ cup scallion, chopped
- 4 oz. cheddar cheese, shredded
- ¼ cup milk
- ¾ cup heavy cream

1. Whisk baking powder with flour, sugar, salt, and butter in a mixing bowl.
2. Beat milk, cream, and all other ingredients in another bowl.
3. Stir in the flour-butter mixture and mix well until it forms a smooth dough.
4. Place this scones dough on a floured surface and spread it into a 7-inch round sheet.
5. Cut this dough sheet into 6 wedges of equal size.
6. Place these wedges in the cooking pan, lined with parchment paper.
7. Transfer the pan to the 2nd rack position of Air fryer oven and close the door.
8. Select the "Bake" Mode using FUNCTION +/- buttons and select Rack Level 2.
9. Set its cooking time to 25 minutes and temperature to 400 °F, then press "START/ STOP" to initiate cooking.
10. When baked, serve the scones with morning eggs.

French Toast Casserole

Prep Time: 10 minutes | Cook time: 12 minutes | Serves 6

- 3 large eggs
- 1 cup whole milk
- ¼ tsp kosher salt or ⅛ tsp fine salt
- 1 tbsp pure maple syrup
- 1 tsp vanilla
- ¼ tsp cinnamon
- 3 cups (1-inch) stale bread cubes (3 to 4 slices)
- 1 tbsp unsalted butter, at room temperature

1. In a medium bowl, whisk the eggs until the yolks and whites are completely mixed. Add the milk, salt, maple syrup, vanilla, and cinnamon and whisk to combine. Add the bread cubes and gently stir to coat with the egg mixture. Let sit for 2 to 3 minutes so the bread absorbs some of the custard, then gently stir again.
2. Grease the bottom of the sheet pan with the butter. Pour the bread mixture onto the pan, spreading it out evenly.
3. Select AIR ROAST, set temperature to 350°F, and set time to 12 minutes. Select START/PAUSE to begin preheating.
4. Once the unit has preheated, slide the pan into the oven.
5. After about 10 minutes, remove the pan and check the casserole. The top should be browned and the middle of the casserole just set. If more time is needed, return the pan to the oven and continue cooking.
6. When cooking is complete, serve warm with additional butter and maple syrup, if desired.

Chapter 3

Snacks and Appetizer Recipes

Cheesy Broccoli Bites

Prep time: 5 minutes | Cook time: 12 minutes |Serves 5

- 1 cup broccoli florets
- 1 egg, beaten
- ¾ cup cheddar cheese, grated
- 2 tbsp Parmesan cheese, grated
- ¾ cup panko breadcrumbs
- Salt and freshly ground black pepper, as needed

1. In a food processor, add the broccoli and pulse until finely crumbled.
2. In a large bowl, mix together the broccoli and remaining ingredients.
3. Make small equal-sized balls from the mixture.
4. Press AIR OVEN MODE button of Air Fry Oven and turn the dial to select "Air Fry" mode.
5. Press TIME/SLICES button and again turn the dial to set the cooking time to 12 minutes.
6. Now push TEMP/SHADE button and rotate the dial to set the temperature at 350 °F.
7. Press "Start/Stop" button to start.
8. When the unit beeps to show that it is preheated, open the oven door.
9. Arrange the broccoli balls into the air fry basket and insert in the oven.
10. When cooking time is completed, open the oven door and transfer the broccoli bites onto a platter.
11. Serve warm.

Cheesy Sweet Onion Dip

Prep time: 5 minutes | Cook time: 25 minutes |Serves 8

- 1/2 cup mayonnaise
- 2 sweet onion, diced
- 4 oz cream cheese, softened
- 3 cups cheddar cheese, shredded

1. Add all ingredients into the bowl and mix until well combined.
2. Pour mixture into the baking dish.
3. Select bake mode then set the temperature to 375°F and time for 25 minutes. Press start.
4. Once the oven is preheated then place the baking dish into the oven.
5. Serve and enjoy.

Spicy Spinach Chips

Prep time: 10 minutes | Cook time: 10 minutes | Serves 4

- 2 cups fresh spinach leaves, torn into bite-sized pieces
- ½ tbsp coconut oil, melted
- ⅛ tsp garlic powder
- salt, as required

1. In a large bowl and mix together all the ingredients.
2. Arrange the spinach pieces onto the greased sheet pan.
3. Press "Power" button of Air Fry Oven and turn the dial to select "Air Fry" mode.
4. Press TIME/SLICE button and again turn the dial to set the cooking time to 10 minutes
5. Now push TEMP/DARKNESS button and rotate the dial to set the temperature at 300 °F.
6. Press "Start/Pause" button to start.
7. When the unit beeps to show that it is preheated, open the oven door.
8. Insert the sheet pan in oven.
9. Toss the spinach chips once halfway through.
10. When cooking time is completed, open the oven door and transfer the spinach chips onto a platter.
11. Serve warm.

Eggplant Fries

Prep time: 15 minutes. | Cook time: 10 minutes. | Serves 4

- 2 large eggs
- ½ cup grated Parmesan cheese
- ½ cup toasted wheat germ
- 1 tsp Italian seasoning
- ¾ tsp garlic salt
- 1 (1¼-pound) eggplant, peeled
- cooking spray
- 1 cup meatless pasta sauce, warmed

1. Cut the eggplant into sticks.
2. Mix parmesan cheese, wheat germ, seasoning, and garlic salt in a bowl.
3. Coat the eggplant sticks with the parmesan mixture.
4. Place the eggplant fries in the air fry basket and spray them with cooking spray.
5. Transfer the basket to the Air Fry Oven and close the door.
6. Select "Air Fry" mode by rotating the dial.
7. Press the TIME/SLICE button and change the value to 10 minutes.
8. Press the TEMP/DARKNESS button and change the value to 375 °F.
9. Press Start/Pause to begin cooking.
10. Serve warm with marinara sauce.

Crispy Avocado Fries

Prep time: 5 minutes | Cook time: 7 minutes |Serves 2

- ¼ cup all-purpose flour
- Salt and ground black pepper, as required
- 1 egg
- 1 tsp water
- ½ cup panko breadcrumbs
- 1 avocado, peeled, pitted, and sliced into 8 pieces
- Non-stick cooking spray

1. In a shallow bowl, mix the flour, salt, and black pepper together.
2. In a second bowl, mix well egg and water.
3. In a third bowl, put the breadcrumbs.
4. Coat the avocado slices with flour mixture, then dip into egg mixture and finally, coat evenly with the breadcrumbs.
5. Now, spray the avocado slices evenly with cooking spray.
6. Press AIR OVEN MODE button of Air Fry Oven and turn the dial to select "Air Fry" mode.
7. Press TIME/SLICES button and again turn the dial to set the cooking time to 7 minutes.
8. Now push TEMP/SHADE button and rotate the dial to set the temperature at 400 °F.
9. Press "Start/Stop" button to start.
10. When the unit beeps to show that it is preheated, open the oven door.
11. Arrange the avocado fries into the air fry basket and insert in the oven.
12. When cooking time is completed, open the oven door and transfer the avocado fries onto a platter.
13. Serve warm.

Whole Artichoke Hearts

Prep time: 5 minutes | Cook time: 8 minutes | Serves 14

- 14 whole artichoke hearts, packed in water
- 1 egg
- ½ cup all-purpose flour
- ⅓ cup panko bread crumbs
- 1 tsp Italian seasoning
- Cooking spray

1. Squeeze excess water from the artichoke hearts and place them on paper towels to dry.
2. In a small bowl, beat the egg. In another small bowl, place the flour. In a third small bowl, combine the bread crumbs and Italian seasoning, and stir.
3. Spritz the air fryer basket with cooking spray.
4. Dip the artichoke hearts in the flour, then the egg, and then the bread crumb mixture.
5. Place the breaded artichoke hearts in the air fryer basket. Spray them with cooking spray.
6. Select the AIR FRY function and cook at 380°F for 8 minutes, or until the artichoke hearts have browned and are crisp, flipping once halfway through.
7. Let cool for 5 minutes before serving.

Nutella Banana Pastries

Prep time: 15 minutes | Cook time: 12 minutes | Serves 4

- 1 puff pastry sheet
- ½ cup Nutella
- 2 bananas, peeled and sliced

1. Cut the pastry sheet into 4 equal-sized squares.
2. Spread the Nutella on each square of pastry evenly.
3. Divide the banana slices over Nutella.
4. Fold each square into a triangle and with wet fingers, slightly press the edges.
5. Then with a fork, press the edges firmly.
6. Press "Power" button of Air Fry Oven and turn the dial to select "Air Fry" mode.
7. Press TIME/SLICE button and again turn the dial to set the cooking time to 12 minutes
8. Now push TEMP/DARKNESS button and rotate the dial to set the temperature at 375 °F.
9. Press "Start/Pause" button to start.
10. When the unit beeps to show that it is preheated, open the oven door.
11. Arrange the pastries into the greased air fry basket and insert in the oven.
12. When cooking time is completed, open the oven door and serve warm.

Puffed Egg Tarts

Prep time: 15 minutes | Cook time: 21 minutes | Serves 4

- ½ (17.3 oz. package) frozen puff pastry, thawed
- ¾ cup Cheddar cheese, shredded
- 4 large eggs
- 1 tbsp fresh parsley, minced

1. Spread the pastry sheet on a floured surface and cut it into 4 squares of equal size.
2. Place the four squares in the sheet pan of the Air Fry Oven .
3. Transfer the sheet to the Air Fry Oven and close the door.
4. Select "Air Fry" mode by rotating the dial.
5. Press the TEMP/DARKNESS button and change the value to 300 °F.
6. Press the TIME/SLICE button and change the value to 10 minutes, then press Start/Pause to begin cooking.
7. Press the center of each pastry square using the back of a metal spoon.
8. Divide cheese into these indentations and crack one egg into each pastry.
9. Return to the oven and close its oven door.
10. Rotate the dial to select the "Air Fry" mode.
11. Press the TIME/SLICE button and again use the dial to set the cooking time to 11 minutes
12. Now Press the TEMP/DARKNESS button and rotate the dial to set the temperature at 350 °F.
13. Garnish the squares with parsley.
14. Serve warm.

Mini Hot Dogs

Prep time: 15 minutes | Cook time: 4 minutes | Serves 8

- 8 oz. refrigerated crescent rolls
- 24 cocktail hot dogs

1. Spread the crescent rolls into 8 triangles and cut each into 3 triangles.
2. Place one mini hot dog at the center of each crescent roll.
3. Wrap the rolls around the hot dog and place them in the air fry basket.
4. Transfer the basket to the Air Fry Oven and close the door.
5. Select "Air Fry" mode by rotating the dial.
6. Press the TIME/SLICE button and change the value to 4 minutes.
7. Press the TEMP/DARKNESS button and change the value to 325 °F.
8. Press Start/Pause to begin cooking.
9. Serve warm.

Cajun Dill Pickle Chips

Prep time: 5 minutes | Cook time: 10 minutes | Makes 16 slices

- ¼ cup all-purpose flour
- ½ cup panko bread crumbs
- 1 large egg, beaten
- 2 tsp Cajun seasoning
- 2 large dill pickles, sliced into 8 rounds each
- Cooking spray

1. Place the all-purpose flour, panko bread crumbs, and egg into 3 separate shallow bowls, then stir the Cajun seasoning into the flour.
2. Dredge each pickle chip in the flour mixture, then the egg, and finally the bread crumbs. Shake off any excess, then place each coated pickle chip on a plate.
3. Spritz the air fryer basket with cooking spray, then place 8 pickle chips in the basket. Select the AIR FRY function and cook at 390°F for 5 minutes, or until crispy and golden brown. Repeat this process with the remaining pickle chips.
4. Remove the chips and allow to slightly cool on a wire rack before serving.

Baked Zucchini Tots

Prep time: 5 minutes | Cook time: 30 minutes |Serves 4

- 1 egg
- 2 cups zucchini, grated & squeezed
- 1/4 tsp onion powder
- 1 tsp Italian seasoning
- 1/2 cup breadcrumbs
- 1/2 cup cheddar cheese, shredded
- Pepper
- Salt

1. Add zucchini and remaining ingredients into the large bowl and mix until well combined.
2. Spray sheet pan with cooking spray.
3. Make small tots from the mixture and place them on a greased sheet pan.
4. Select bake mode then set the temperature to 400°F and time for 30 minutes. Press start.
5. Once the oven is preheated then place the sheet pan into the oven.
6. Serve and enjoy.

Crispy Green Olives

Prep time: 5 minutes | Cook time: 8 minutes | Serves 4

- 1 (5½ oz.) jar pitted green olives
- ½ cup all-purpose flour
- Salt and pepper, to taste
- ½ cup bread crumbs
- 1 egg
- Cooking spray

1. Remove the olives from the jar and dry thoroughly with paper towels.
2. In a small bowl, combine the flour with salt and pepper to taste. Place the bread crumbs in another small bowl. In a third small bowl, beat the egg.
3. Spritz the air fryer basket with cooking spray.
4. Dip the olives in the flour, then the egg, and then the bread crumbs.
5. Place the breaded olives in the air fryer oven. It is okay to stack them. Spray the olives with cooking spray.
6. Select the AIR FRY function and cook at 400°F for 6 minutes. Flip the olives and air fry for an additional 2 minutes, or until brown and crisp.
7. Cool before serving.

Chapter 4

Poultry Recipes

Chicken Potato Bake

Prep time: 5 minutes | Cook time: 25 minutes | Serves 4

- 4 potatoes, diced
- 1 tbsp garlic, minced
- 1.5 tbsp olive oil
- ⅛ tsp salt
- ⅛ tsp pepper
- 1.5 pounds boneless skinless chicken
- ¾ cup mozzarella cheese, shredded
- Parsley, chopped

1. Toss chicken and potatoes with all the spices and oil in a SearPlate.
2. Drizzle the cheese on top of the chicken and potato.
3. Transfer the SearPlate to Air Fry Oven and close the door.
4. Select "Bake" mode by rotating the dial.
5. Press the TIME/SLICES button and change the value to 25 minutes.
6. Press the TEMP/SHADE button and change the value to 375 °F.
7. Press Start/Stop to begin cooking.
8. Serve warm.

Chicken Casserole

Prep time: 5 minutes | Cook time: 25 minutes | Serves 5

- 1 1/4 lbs chicken, cooked and shredded
- 1/2 cup water
- 1/2 cup heavy cream
- 8 oz cream cheese
- 5 oz green beans, chopped
- 1/4 cup mozzarella cheese, shredded
- 1/4 cup parmesan cheese, grated
- 1/2 tsp garlic powder
- Salt

1. In a medium saucepan, heat heavy cream, parmesan cheese, garlic powder, cream cheese, water, and salt over low heat until smooth.
2. Add green beans into the greased baking dish.
3. Spread chicken on top of green beans.
4. Pour cream mixture over chicken and top with mozzarella.
5. Select bake mode then set the temperature to 350°F and time for 25 minutes. Press start.
6. Once the oven is preheated then place the baking dish into the oven.
7. Serve and enjoy.

Spanish Chicken Bake

Prep Time: 15 minutes|Cook Time: 25 minutes|- Serves 4

- ½ onion, quartered
- ½ red onion, quartered
- ½ pound potatoes, quartered
- 4 garlic cloves
- 4 tomatoes, quartered
- ⅛ cup chorizo
- ¼ tsp paprika powder
- 4 chicken thighs, boneless
- ¼ tsp dried oregano
- ½ green bell pepper, julienned
- Salt, to taste
- Black pepper, to taste

1. Toss chicken, veggies, and all the ingredients in a roast tray.
2. Transfer the tray to the 2nd rack position of Air fryer oven and close the door.
3. Select the "Bake" Mode using FUNCTION +/- buttons and select Rack Level 2.
4. Set its cooking time to 25 minutes and temperature to 425 °F, then press "START/STOP" to initiate cooking.
5. Serve warm.

Italian Chicken Breast

Prep time: 5 minutes | Cook time: 45 minutes |Serves 8

- 8 chicken breasts, skinless and boneless
- 3 oz feta cheese, crumbled
- 1 tbsp oregano
- 4 tbsp fresh lemon juice
- Pepper
- Salt

1. Place chicken in a baking dish.
2. Mix together the remaining ingredients and pour over the chicken.
3. Select bake mode then set the temperature to 350°F and time for 45 minutes. Press start.
4. Once the oven is preheated then place the baking dish into the oven.
5. Serve and enjoy.

Cheesy Chicken Cutlets

Prep time: 5 minutes | Cook time: 30 minutes |Serves 2

- 1 large egg
- 6 tbsp flour
- ¾ cup panko breadcrumbs
- 2 tbsp parmesan cheese, grated
- 2 chicken cutlets, skinless and boneless
- ½ tbsp mustard powder
- Salt and black pepper, to taste

1. Take a shallow bowl, add the flour.
2. In a second bowl, crack the egg and beat well.
3. Take a third bowl and mix together breadcrumbs, cheeses, mustard powder, salt and black pepper.
4. Season the chicken with salt and black pepper.
5. Coat the chicken with flour, then dip into beaten egg and then finally coat with the breadcrumbs mixture.
6. Turn on your Air Fry Oven and rotate the knob to select "Air Fry".
7. Select the timer for about 30 minutes and temperature for 355 °F.
8. Grease the air fry basket and place the chicken cutlets into the prepared basket.
9. Remove from the oven and serve on a platter.
10. Serve hot and enjoy!

Golden Chicken Nuggets

Prep time: 10 minutes | Cook time: 10 to 13 minutes | Serves 4

- 1 egg white
- 1 tbsp freshly squeezed lemon juice
- ½ tsp dried basil
- ½ tsp ground paprika
- 1 pound (454 g) low-sodium boneless, skinless chicken breasts, cut into 1½-inch cubes
- ½ cup ground almonds
- 2 slices low-sodium whole-wheat bread, crumbled

1. Select the BAKE function and preheat AIR FRYER OVEN to 400°F.
2. In a shallow bowl, beat the egg white, lemon juice, basil, and paprika with a fork until foamy.
3. Add the chicken and stir to coat.
4. On a plate, mix the almonds and bread crumbs.
5. Toss the chicken cubes in the almond and bread crumb mixture until coated.
6. Bake the nuggets in the air fryer oven, in two batches, for 10 to 13 minutes, or until the chicken reaches an internal temperature of 165°F on a meat thermometer. Serve immediately.

Chicken Wings with Hot Sauce

Prep time: 10 minutes | Cook time: 24 minutes | Serves 4

- 8 tbsp (1 stick) unsalted butter, melted
- ½ cup hot sauce
- 2 tbsp white vinegar
- 2 tsp Worcestershire sauce
- 1 tsp garlic powder
- ½ cup all-purpose flour
- 16 frozen chicken wings

1. In a small saucepan over low heat, combine the butter, hot sauce, vinegar, Worcestershire sauce, and garlic. Mix well and bring to a simmer.
2. Pour the flour into a medium mixing bowl. Dredge the chicken wings in the flour.
3. Place the flour-coated wings into the air fryer basket.
4. Select the AIR FRY function and cook at 370°F for 12 minutes.
5. Using tongs, flip the wings. Air fry for 12 minutes more.
6. Remove the air fryer basket from the oven. Transfer the chicken wings into a large mixing bowl, then pour the sauce over them.
7. Serve and enjoy!

Asian Turkey Meatballs

Prep time: 10 minutes | Cook time: 11 to 14 minutes | Serves 4

- 2 tbsp peanut oil, divided
- 1 small onion, minced
- ¼ cup water chestnuts, finely chopped
- ½ tsp ground ginger
- 2 tbsp low-sodium soy sauce
- ¼ cup panko bread crumbs
- 1 egg, beaten
- 1 pound (454 g) ground turkey

1. Select the BAKE function and preheat AIR FRYER OVEN to 400°F.
2. In a round metal pan, combine 1 tbsp of peanut oil and onion. Bake for 1 to 2 minutes or until crisp and tender. Transfer the onion to a medium bowl.
3. Add the water chestnuts, ground ginger, soy sauce, and bread crumbs to the onion and mix well. Add egg and stir well. Mix in the ground turkey until combined.
4. Form the mixture into 1-inch meatballs. Drizzle the remaining 1 tbsp of oil over the meatballs.
5. Bake the meatballs in the pan in batches for 10 to 12 minutes or until they are 165°F on a meat thermometer. Rest for 5 minutes before serving.

Chicken Breast Pita Sandwich

Prep time: 10 minutes | Cook time: 9 to 11 minutes | Serves 4

- 2 boneless, skinless chicken breasts, cut into 1-inch cubes
- 1 small red onion, sliced
- 1 red bell pepper, sliced
- ⅓ cup Italian salad dressing, divided
- ½ tsp dried thyme
- 4 pita pockets, split
- 2 cups torn butter lettuce
- 1 cup chopped cherry tomatoes

1. Select the BAKE function and preheat AIR FRYER OVEN to 380°F.
2. Place the chicken, onion, and bell pepper in the air fryer basket. Drizzle with 1 tbsp of the Italian salad dressing, add the thyme, and toss.
3. Bake for 9 to 11 minutes, or until the chicken is 165°F on a food thermometer, stirring once during cooking time.
4. Transfer the chicken and vegetables to a bowl and toss with the remaining salad dressing.
5. Assemble sandwiches with the pita pockets, butter lettuce, and cherry tomatoes. Serve immediately.

Herbed Duck Breast

Prep time: 5 minutes | Cook time: 20 minutes |Serves 2

- 1 duck breast
- Olive oil cooking spray
- ½ tbsp fresh thyme, chopped
- ½ tbsp fresh rosemary, chopped
- 1 cup chicken broth
- 1 tbsp fresh lemon juice
- Salt and ground black pepper, as required

1. Spray the duck breast with cooking spray evenly.
2. In a bowl, mix well the remaining ingredients.
3. Add the duck breast and coat with the marinade generously.
4. Refrigerate, covered for about 4 hours.
5. With a piece of foil, cover the duck breast
6. Press AIR OVEN MODE button of Air Fry Oven and turn the dial to select "Air Fry" mode.
7. Press TIME/SLICES button and again turn the dial to set the cooking time to 15 minutes.
8. Now push TEMP/SHADE button and rotate the dial to set the temperature at 390 °F.
9. Press "Start/Stop" button to start.
10. When the unit beeps to show that it is preheated, open the oven door and grease the air fry basket.
11. Place the duck breast into the prepared air fry basket and insert in the oven.
12. After 15 minutes of cooking, set the temperature to 355 °F for 5 minutes.
13. When cooking time is completed, open the oven door and serve hot.

Lemony Whole Chicken

Prep time: 5 minutes | Cook time: 1 hour 20 minutes |Serves 8

- 1 whole chicken, neck and giblets removed
- Salt and ground black pepper, as required
- 2 fresh rosemary sprigs
- 1 small onion, peeled and quartered
- 1 garlic clove, peeled and cut in half
- 4 lemon zest slices
- 1 tbsp extra-virgin olive oil
- 1 tbsp fresh lemon juice

1. Rub the inside and outside of chicken with salt and black pepper evenly.
2. Place the rosemary sprigs, onion quarters, garlic halves and lemon zest in the cavity of the chicken.
3. With kitchen twine, tie off wings and legs.
4. Arrange the chicken onto a greased SearPlate and drizzle with oil and lemon juice.
5. Press AIR OVEN MODE button of Air Fry Oven and turn the dial to select "Bake" mode.
6. Press TIME/SLICES button and again turn the dial to set the cooking time to 20 minutes.
7. Now push TEMP/SHADE button and rotate the dial to set the temperature at 400 °F.
8. Press "Start/Stop" button to start.
9. When the unit beeps to show that it is preheated, open the oven door.
10. Insert the SearPlate in the oven.
11. After 20 minutes of cooking, set the temperature to 375 °F for 60 minutes.
12. When cooking time is completed, open the oven door and place the chicken onto a platter for about 10 minutes before carving.
13. Cut into desired sized pieces and serve.

Chapter 5

Beef, Pork and Lamb Recipes

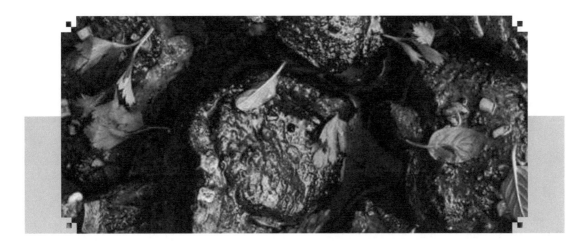

Garlicky Lamb Steaks

Prep time: 5 minutes | Cook time: 15 minutes |Serves 4

- ½ onion, roughly chopped
- 5 garlic cloves, peeled
- 1 tbsp fresh ginger, peeled
- 1 tsp ground fennel
- ½ tsp ground cumin
- ½ tsp ground cinnamon
- ½ tsp cayenne pepper
- Salt and ground black pepper, as required
- 1½ pounds boneless lamb sirloin steaks

1. In a blender, add the onion, garlic, ginger, and spices and pulse until smooth.
2. Transfer the mixture into a large bowl.
3. Add the lamb steaks and coat with the mixture generously.
4. Refrigerate to marinate for about 24 hours.
5. Press AIR OVEN MODE button of Air Fry Oven and turn the dial to select "Air Fry" mode.
6. Press TIME/SLICES button and again turn the dial to set the cooking time to 15 minutes.
7. Now push TEMP/SHADE button and rotate the dial to set the temperature at 330 °F.
8. Press "Start/Stop" button to start.
9. When the unit beeps to show that it is preheated, open the oven door and grease the air fry basket.
10. Place the lamb steaks into the prepared air fry basket and insert in the oven.
11. Flip the steaks once halfway through.
12. When cooking time is completed, open the oven door and serve hot.

Tarragon Beef Shanks

Prep time: 5 minutes | Cook time: 15 minutes |Serves 4

- 2 tbsp olive oil
- 2 pounds beef shank
- Salt and black pepper to taste
- 1 onion, diced
- 2 stalks celery, diced
- 1 cup Marsala wine
- 2 tbsp dried tarragon

1. Place the beef shanks in a baking pan.
2. Whisk the rest of the ingredients in a bowl and pour over the shanks.
3. Place these shanks in the air fry basket.
4. Transfer the basket to Air Fry Oven and close the door.
5. Select "Air Fry" mode by rotating the dial.
6. Press the TIME/SLICES button and change the value to 15 minutes.
7. Press the TEMP/SHADE button and change the value to 375 °F.
8. Press Start/Stop to begin cooking.
9. Serve warm.

Herbed Chuck Roast

Prep time: 5 minutes | Cook time: 45 minutes |Serves 6

- 1 beef chuck roast
- 1 tbsp olive oil
- 1 tsp dried rosemary, crushed
- 1 tsp dried thyme, crushed
- Salt, as required

1. In a bowl, add the oil, herbs and salt and mix well.
2. Coat the beef roast with herb mixture generously.
3. Arrange the beef roast onto the greased SearPlate.
4. Press AIR OVEN MODE button of Air Fry Oven and turn the dial to select "Air Fry" mode.
5. Press TIME/SLICES button and again turn the dial to set the cooking time to 45 minutes.
6. Now push TEMP/SHADE button and rotate the dial to set the temperature at 360 °F.
7. Press "Start/Stop" button to start.
8. When the unit beeps to show that it is preheated, open the oven door and insert the SearPlate in the oven.
9. When cooking time is completed, open the oven door and place the roast onto a cutting board.
10. With a piece of foil, cover the beef roast for about 20 minutes before slicing.
11. With a sharp knife, cut the beef roast into desired size slices and serve.

Tasty Chicken Drumsticks

Prep time: 5 minutes | Cook time: 20 minutes |Serves 4

- 4 chicken drumsticks
- 3/4 cup teriyaki sauce
- 4 tbsp green onion, chopped
- 1 tbsp sesame seeds, toasted

1. Select air fry mode set the temperature to 360°F and set the timer to 20 minutes. Press the setting dial to preheat.
2. Add chicken drumsticks and teriyaki sauce into the zip-lock bag. Seal bag and place in refrigerator for 1 hour.
3. Arrange marinated chicken drumsticks in the air fryer basket.
4. Once the unit is preheated, open the door, and place the air fryer basket on the top level of the oven, and close the door.
5. Garnish with green onion and sprinkle with sesame seeds.
6. Serve and enjoy.

Greek Lamb Rib Rack

Prep time: 5 minutes | Cook time: 10 minutes | Serves 4

- ¼ cup freshly squeezed lemon juice
- 1 tsp oregano
- 2 tsp minced fresh rosemary
- 1 tsp minced fresh thyme
- 2 tbsp minced garlic
- Salt and freshly ground black pepper, to taste
- 2 to 4 tbsp olive oil
- 1 lamb rib rack (7 to 8 ribs)

1. Select the ROAST function and preheat AIR FRYER OVEN to 360°F.
2. In a small mixing bowl, combine the lemon juice, oregano, rosemary, thyme, garlic, salt, pepper, and olive oil and mix well.
3. Rub the mixture over the lamb, covering all the meat. Put the rack of lamb in the air fryer oven. Roast for 10 minutes. Flip the rack halfway through.
4. After 10 minutes, measure the internal temperature of the rack of lamb reaches at least 145°F.
5. Serve immediately.

Chimichurri Flank Steak

Prep time: 5 minutes | Cook time: 12 minutes | Serves 1

- 1 flank steak
- Salt and ground black pepper, to taste
- 2 avocados
- 2 tbsp butter, melted
- ½ cup chimichurri sauce

1. Rub the flank steak with salt and pepper to taste and leave to sit for 20 minutes.
2. Halve the avocados and take out the pits. Spoon the flesh into a bowl and mash with a fork. Mix in the melted butter and chimichurri sauce, making sure everything is well combined.
3. Put the steak in the air fryer basket. Select the AIR FRY function and cook at 400°F for 6 minutes. Flip over and allow to air fry for another 6 minutes.
4. Serve the steak with the avocado butter.

Lamb Kebabs

Prep time: 5 minutes | Cook time: 20 minutes |Serves 4

- 18 oz. lamb mince
- 1 tsp chili powder
- 1 tsp cumin powder
- 1 egg
- 2 oz. onion, chopped
- 2 tsp sesame oil

1. Whisk onion with egg, chili powder, oil, cumin powder, and salt in a bowl.
2. Add lamb to coat well, then thread it on the skewers.
3. Place these lamb skewers in the air fry basket.
4. Transfer the basket to Air Fry Oven and close the door.
5. Select "Air Fry" mode by rotating the dial.
6. Press the TIME/SLICES button and change the value to 20 minutes.
7. Press the TEMP/SHADE button and change the value to 395 °F.
8. Press Start/Stop to begin cooking.
9. Serve warm.

Beef Spring Rolls

Prep time: 10 minutes | Cook time: 8 minutes | Serves 20

- ⅓ cup noodles
- 1 cup ground beef
- 1 tsp soy sauce
- 1 cup fresh mix vegetables
- 3 garlic cloves, minced
- 1 small onion, diced
- 1 tbsp sesame oil
- 1 packet spring roll sheets
- 2 tbsp cold water

1. Cook the noodle in enough hot water to soften them up, drain them and snip them to make them shorter.
2. In a frying pan over medium heat, cook the beef, soy sauce, mixed vegetables, garlic, and onion in sesame oil until the beef is cooked through. Take the pan off the heat and throw in the noodles. Mix well to incorporate everything.
3. Unroll a spring roll sheet and lay it flat. Scatter the filling diagonally across it and roll it up, brushing the edges lightly with water to act as an adhesive. Repeat until you have used up all the sheets and the filling.
4. Coat each spring roll with a light brushing of oil and transfer to the air fryer oven.
5. Select the AIR FRY function and cook at 350°F for 8 minutes.
6. Serve hot.

Savory Pork Roast

Prep time: 5 minutes | Cook time: 1 hour |Serves 3

- ¼ tsp dried thyme
- 1 tbsp fresh rosemary, divided
- 1 tsp garlic salt
- ⅛ tsp black pepper, freshly ground
- 1½ pounds pork loin roast, boneless

1. Turn on your Air Fry Oven and rotate the knob to select "Air Roast".
2. Preheat by selecting the timer for 3 minutes and temperature for 350 °F.
3. Take a bowl mix well rosemary, garlic salt, thyme, and pepper together.
4. Now add pork to coat well.
5. Take a dish and place coated pork on it.
6. Roast pork for about an hour in preheated Air Fry Oven at 350 °F.
7. Serve and enjoy!

Marinated Steak Bites

Prep time: 5 minutes | Cook time: 10 minutes |Serves 6

- 1 lb ribeye steak, cut into pieces
- 1/4 tsp red pepper flakes
- 1/2 tsp garlic powder
- 1 tbsp lemon juice
- 1 tbsp lemon zest
- 1 stick butter, melted
- 1 tbsp parsley, chopped
- 1/2 tsp Worcestershire sauce
- 1/2 tbsp Dijon mustard
- Pepper
- Salt

1. Select air fry mode set the temperature to 400°F and set the timer to 10 minutes. Press the setting dial to preheat.
2. Add steak pieces and remaining ingredients into the bowl and mix well.
3. Cover and set aside for 30 minutes.
4. Remove steak pieces from the marinade and place into the air fryer basket.
5. Once the unit is preheated, open the door, and place the air fryer basket on the top level of the oven, and close the door.
6. Serve and enjoy.

Roasted Lamb Leg

Prep time: 5 minutes | Cook time: 75 minutes |Serves 4

- 2 ½ lbs. lamb leg roast, slits carved
- 1 tbsp of olive oil
- 2 garlic cloves, sliced into smaller slithers
- 1 tbsp of dried rosemary
- Cracked Himalayan rock salt to taste
- Ground peppercorns to taste

1. Make the cuts in the lamb roast and insert them with garlic. Season with oil.
2. Sprinkle the lamb roast with kosher salt, rosemary, and ground black pepper.
3. Place the lamb roast on the Air Crisp Basket.
4. Preheat the Air Fry Oven by selecting the "AIR ROAST" mode.
5. Adjust the temperature to 380 °F, set time to 75 minutes.
6. Open the door and transfer to the Air Fry Oven.
7. Remove and allow to rest.
8. Serve and enjoy.

Rosemary Beef Roast

Prep time: 5 minutes | Cook time: 45 minutes |Serves 6

- 2 lbs beef roast
- 1 tsp rosemary
- 1 tbsp olive oil
- 1 tsp salt

1. Mix together oil, rosemary, pepper, and salt and rub all over the meat.
2. Place beef roast in an air fryer basket.
3. Select air fry then set the temperature to 360 °F and time for 45 minutes. Press start.
4. Once the oven is preheated then place the basket into the top rails of the oven.
5. Serve and enjoy.

Double Cheese Beef Meatballs

Prep time: 5 minutes | Cook time: 18 minutes | Serves 6

- 1 pound ground beef
- ½ cup grated Parmesan cheese
- 1 tbsp minced garlic
- ½ cup Mozzarella cheese
- 1 tsp freshly ground pepper

1. In a bowl, mix all the ingredients together.
2. Roll the meat mixture into 5 generous meatballs. Arrange in the air fryer basket.
3. Select the AIR FRY function and cook at 400°F for 18 minutes.
4. Serve immediately.

Chapter 6

Fish and Seafood Recipes

Garlic Butter Salmon Bites

Prep time: 5 minutes | Cook time: 10 minutes |Serves 2

- 1 tbsp lemon juice
- 2 tbsp butter
- ½ tbsp garlic, minced
- ½ tsp pepper
- 4 oz. salmon
- ½ tsp salt
- ½ tbsp apple cider or rice vinegar

1. Take a large bowl and add everything except salmon and whisk together until well combined.
2. Slice the salmon into small cubes and marinade them into the mixture.
3. Cover the bowl with plastic wrap and refrigerate it for about an hour.
4. Now, spread out the marinated salmon cubes into the air fry basket.
5. Turn on your Air Fry Oven and rotate the knob to select "Air Fry".
6. Select the timer for 10 minutes and temperature for 350 °F.
7. Wait till the salmon is finely cooked.
8. Serve and enjoy!

Herbed Shrimp

Prep time: 5 minutes | Cook time: 7 minutes |Serves 3

- 4 tbsp salted butter, melted
- 1 tbsp fresh lemon juice
- 1 tbsp garlic, minced
- 2 tsp red pepper flakes, crushed
- 1 pound shrimp, peeled and deveined
- 2 tbsp fresh basil, chopped
- 1 tbsp fresh chives, chopped
- 2 tbsp chicken broth

1. In a 7-inch round baking pan, place butter, lemon juice, garlic, and red pepper flakes and mix well.
2. Press AIR OVEN MODE button of Air Fry Oven and turn the dial to select the "Air Fry" mode.
3. Press TIME/SLICES button and again turn the dial to set the cooking time to 7 minutes.
4. Now push TEMP/SHADE button and rotate the dial to set the temperature at 325 °F.
5. Press "Start/Stop" button to start.
6. When the unit beeps to show that it is preheated, open the oven door and insert the SearPlate in the oven.
7. After 2 minutes of cooking in the SearPlate, stir in the shrimp, basil, chives, and broth.
8. When cooking time is completed, open the oven door and stir the mixture.
9. Serve hot.

Bacon-Wrapped Scallops with Salad

Prep time: 10 minutes | Cook time: 12 minutes | Serves 4

- 12 slices bacon
- 24 large sea scallops, tendons removed
- 1 tsp plus 2 tbsp extra-virgin olive oil, divided
- Salt and pepper, to taste
- 1 tbsp cider vinegar
- 1 tsp Dijon mustard
- 5 oz. baby spinach
- 1 fennel bulb, stalks discarded, bulb halved, cored, and sliced thin
- 5 oz. raspberries

1. Select the BAKE function and preheat AIR FRYER OVEN to 350°F.
2. Line large plate with 4 layers of paper towels and arrange 6 slices bacon over towels in a single layer. Top with 4 more layers of paper towels and remaining 6 slices bacon. Cover with 2 layers of paper towels, place a second large plate on top, and press gently to flatten. Microwave until fat begins to render but bacon is still pliable, about 5 minutes.
3. Pat scallops dry with paper towels and toss with 1 tsp oil, ⅛ tsp salt, and ⅛ tsp pepper in a bowl until evenly coated. Arrange 2 scallops side to side, flat side down, on the cutting board. Starting at narrow end, wrap 1 slice bacon tightly around sides of scallop bundle. (Bacon should overlap slightly; trim excess as needed.) Thread scallop bundle onto skewer through bacon. Repeat with remaining scallops and bacon, threading 2 bundles onto each skewer.
4. Arrange 3 skewers in air fryer basket, parallel to each other and spaced evenly apart. Arrange remaining 3 skewers on top, perpendicular to the bottom layer. Bake until bacon is crisp and scallops are firm and centers are opaque, 12 to 16 minutes, flipping and rotating skewers halfway through cooking.
5. Meanwhile, whisk remaining 2 tbsp oil, vinegar, mustard, ⅛ tsp salt, and ⅛ tsp pepper in large serving bowl until combined. Add spinach, fennel, and raspberries and gently toss to coat. Serve skewers with salad.

Air Fried Fish Sticks

Prep time: 5 minutes | Cook time: 15 minutes |Serves 1

- ½ pound fish fillets
- ¼ tsp ground black pepper, divided
- 1 egg
- ¼ cup flour
- ½ tsp salt, divided
- ½ cup breadcrumbs, dried

1. Take a bowl and add flour, salt and pepper.
2. In a second bowl, whisk the egg. In another bowl, add breadcrumbs.
3. Dredge the fish in flour, then dip in egg and lastly coat with breadcrumbs.
4. Once they are done, put them in an air fry basket.
5. Turn on your Air Fry Oven and rotate the knob to select "Air Fry".
6. Select the timer for about 10 to 15 minutes and temperature for 400 °F.
7. Serve and enjoy!

Lime Blackened Shrimp Tacos

Prep time: 10 minutes | Cook time: 10 to 15 minutes | Serves 4

- 12 oz. medium shrimp, deveined, with tails off
- 1 tsp olive oil
- 1 to 2 tsp Blackened seasoning
- 8 corn tortillas, warmed
- 1 (14 oz.) bag coleslaw mix
- 2 limes, cut in half
- Cooking spray

1. Spray the air fryer basket lightly with cooking spray.
2. Dry the shrimp with a paper towel to remove excess water.
3. In a medium bowl, toss the shrimp with olive oil and Blackened seasoning.
4. Place the shrimp in the air fryer basket. Select the AIR FRY function and cook at 400°F for 5 minutes. Shake the basket, lightly spray with cooking spray, and cook until the shrimp are cooked through and starting to brown, 5 to 10 more minutes.
5. Fill each tortilla with the coleslaw mix and top with the blackened shrimp. Squeeze fresh lime juice over top and serve.

Prawns in Butter Sauce

Prep Time: 15 minutes|Cook Time: 6 minutes|-Serves 2

- ½ pound large prawns, peeled and deveined
- 1 large garlic clove, minced
- 1 tbsp butter, melted
- 1 tsp fresh lemon zest, grated

1. In a bowl, add all the ingredients and toss to coat well.
2. Set aside at room temperature for about 30 minutes.
3. Arrange the prawn mixture into a baking pan.
4. Press "Power" button of Air fryer oven and select "Bake" function.
5. Press TEMP/SHADE +/- buttons to set the temperature at 450 °F.
6. Now press TIME/SLICES +/- buttons to set the cooking time to 6 minutes.
7. Press "START/STOP" button to start.
8. When the unit beeps to show that it is preheated, open the lid.
9. Arrange the pan over the wire rack and insert in the oven.
10. When cooking time is completed, open the lid and serve immediately.

New Orleans Crab Cakes

Prep time: 10 minutes | Cook time: 8 to 10 minutes | Serves 4

- 1¼ cups bread crumbs
- 2 tsp Creole Seasoning
- 1 tsp dry mustard
- 1 tsp salt
- 1 tsp freshly ground black pepper
- 1½ cups crab meat
- 2 large eggs, beaten
- 1 tsp butter, melted
- ⅓ cup minced onion
- Cooking spray
- Pecan Tartar Sauce, for serving

1. Line the air fryer basket with parchment paper.
2. In a medium bowl, whisk the bread crumbs, Creole Seasoning, dry mustard, salt, and pepper until blended. Add the crab meat, eggs, butter, and onion. Stir until blended. Shape the crab mixture into 8 patties.
3. Place the crab cakes on the parchment and spritz with oil.
4. Select the AIR FRY function and cook at 350°F for 4 minutes. Flip the cakes, spritz them with oil, and air fry for 4 to 6 minutes more until the outsides are firm and a fork inserted into the center comes out clean. Serve with the Pecan Tartar Sauce.

Chapter 7

Vegetables and Sides Recipes

Herbed Bell Peppers

Prep time: 5 minutes | Cook time: 8 minutes
|Serves 4

- 1½ pounds mixed bell peppers, seeded and sliced
- 1 small onion, sliced
- ½ tsp dried thyme, crushed
- ½ tsp dried savory, crushed
- Salt and ground black pepper, as required
- 2 tbsp butter, melted

1. In a bowl, add the bell peppers, onion, herbs, salt and black pepper and toss to coat well.
2. Press AIR OVEN MODE button of Air Fry Oven and turn the dial to select "Air Fry" mode.
3. Press TIME/SLICES button and again turn the dial to set the cooking time to 8 minutes.
4. Now push TEMP/SHADE button and rotate the dial to set the temperature at 360 °F.
5. Press "Start/Stop" button to start.
6. When the unit beeps to show that it is preheated, open the oven door.
7. Arrange the bell peppers into the air fry basket and insert in the oven.
8. When cooking time is completed, open the oven door and transfer the bell peppers into a bowl.
9. Drizzle with butter and serve immediately.

Beans & Veggie Burgers

Prep time: 5 minutes | Cook time: 22 minutes
|Serves 4

- 1 cup cooked black beans
- 2 cups boiled potatoes, peeled, and mashed
- 1 cup fresh spinach, chopped
- 1 cup fresh mushrooms, chopped
- 2 tsp Chile lime seasoning
- Olive oil cooking spray

1. In a large bowl, add the beans, potatoes, spinach, mushrooms, and seasoning and with your hands, mix until well combined.
2. Make 4 equal-sized patties from the mixture.
3. Spray the patties with cooking spray evenly.
4. Press AIR OVEN MODE button of Air Fry Oven and turn the dial to select "Air Fry" mode.
5. Press TIME/SLICES button and again turn the dial to set the cooking time to 22 minutes.
6. Now push TEMP/SHADE button and rotate the dial to set the temperature at 370 °F.
7. Press "Start/Stop" button to start.
8. When the unit beeps to show that it is preheated, open the oven door.
9. Arrange the patties in the greased air fry basket and insert in the oven.
10. Flip the patties once after 12 minutes.
11. When cooking time is completed, open the oven door and remove the air fry basket from the oven.

Sweet & Spicy Parsnips

Prep time: 5 minutes | Cook time: 44 minutes |Serves 5

- 1½ pound parsnip, peeled and cut into chunks
- 1 tbsp butter, melted
- 2 tbsp honey
- 1 tbsp dried parsley flakes, crushed
- ¼ tsp red pepper flakes, crushed
- Salt and ground black pepper, to taste

1. In a large bowl, mix the parsnips and butter.
2. Select the "AIR CRISP" function and the temperature at 355 °F on your Air Fry Oven .
3. Set the cooking time to 44 minutes.
4. Press the "START/PAUSE" button to start.
5. Arrange the squash chunks into the greased Air Crisp Basket and insert them in the oven. Meanwhile, in another large bowl, mix the remaining ingredients.
6. After 40 minutes of cooking, press the "START/PAUSE" button to pause the unit. Transfer the parsnip chunks into the bowl of honey mixture and toss to coat well.
7. Again, arrange the parsnip chunks into the Air Crisp Basket and insert them in the oven. When cooking time is completed, open the door and serve hot.

Tomato Zucchini Bake

Prep time: 5 minutes | Cook time: 30 minutes |Serves 6

- 3 tomatoes, sliced
- 4 medium zucchinis, sliced
- 1 cup parmesan cheese, shredded
- 1 tbsp olive oil
- Pepper
- Salt

1. Arrange sliced tomatoes and zucchinis in the baking dish.
2. Drizzle with olive oil and season with pepper and salt.
3. Sprinkle parmesan cheese on top of vegetables.
4. Select bake mode then set the temperature to 350°F and time for 30 minutes. Press start.
5. Once the oven is preheated then place the baking dish into the oven.
6. Serve and enjoy.

Sweet & Tangy Mushrooms

Prep time: 5 minutes | Cook time: 23minutes |Serves 4

- ¼ cup soy sauce
- ¼ cup honey
- ¼ cup balsamic vinegar
- 2 garlic cloves, chopped finely
- ½ tsp red pepper flakes, crushed
- 18 oz. cremini mushrooms, halved

1. In a bowl, place the soy sauce, honey, vinegar, garlic, and red pepper flakes and mix well. Set aside.
2. Place the mushroom into the greased sheet pan in a single layer.
3. Select "BAKE" mode and set the cooking time to 15 minutes on your Air Fry Oven .
4. Set the temperature at 350 °F.
5. Press the "START/PAUSE" button to start.
6. When the unit beeps to show that it is preheated, open the door. Insert the sheet pan into the oven.
7. After 8 minutes of cooking, place the honey mixture in a sheet pan and toss to coat well.
8. When the unit beeps to show that cooking time is completed, press the "Power" button to stop cooking and open the door.
9. Serve hot.

Asparagus with Garlic and Parmesan

Prep Time: 5 minutes |Cook Time: 10 minutes |Serves 4

- 1 bundle asparagus
- 1 tsp olive oil
- ⅛ tsp garlic salt
- 1 tbsp parmesan cheese
- Pepper to taste

1. Clean the asparagus and dry it. To remove the woody stalks, cut 1 inch off the bottom.
2. In a sheet pan, arrange asparagus in a single layer and spray with oil.
3. On top of the asparagus, evenly sprinkle garlic salt. Season with salt and pepper, then sprinkle with Parmesan cheese.
4. Turn on Air fryer oven and select "Air Fry".
5. Select the timer for 10 minutes and the temperature for 350 °F.
6. When the unit beeps to signify it has preheated, open the oven and place the sheet pan onto Level 3 in oven. Close the oven and let it cook.
7. Enjoy right away.

Smoky Wax Beans

Prep time: 10 minutes | Cook time: 7 minutes | Serves 4

- ½ cup flour
- 1 tsp smoky chipotle powder
- ½ tsp ground black pepper
- 1 tsp sea salt flakes
- 2 eggs, beaten
- ½ cup crushed saltines
- 10 oz. (283 g) wax beans
- Cooking spray

1. Combine the flour, chipotle powder, black pepper, and salt in a bowl. Put the eggs in a second bowl. Put the crushed saltines in a third bowl.
2. Wash the beans with cold water and discard any tough strings.
3. Coat the beans with the flour mixture, before dipping them into the beaten egg. Cover them with the crushed saltines.
4. Spritz the beans with cooking spray.
5. Select the AIR FRY function and cook at 360°F for 4 minutes. Give the air fryer basket a good shake and continue to air fry for 3 minutes. Serve hot.

Rosemary Green Beans

Prep time: 5 minutes | Cook time: 5 minutes | Serves 1

- 1 tbsp butter, melted
- 2 tbsp rosemary
- ½ tsp salt
- 3 cloves garlic, minced
- ¾ cup chopped green beans

1. Combine the melted butter with the rosemary, salt, and minced garlic. Toss in the green beans, coating them well.
2. Select the AIR FRY function and cook at 390°F for 5 minutes.
3. Serve immediately.

Wine Braised Mushrooms

Prep Time: 10 minutes|Cook Time: 32 minutes|Serves 6

- 1 tbsp butter
- 2 tsp Herbs de Provence
- ½ tsp garlic powder
- 2 pounds fresh mushrooms, quartered
- 2 tbsp white wine

1. In a frying pan, mix together the butter, Herbs de Provence, and garlic powder over medium–low heat and stir fry for about 2 minutes.
2. Stir in the mushrooms and remove from the heat.
3. Transfer the mushroom mixture into a baking pan.
4. Press "Power" button of Air fryer oven and select "Air Fry" function.
5. Press TEMP/SHADE +/- buttons to set the temperature at 320 °F.
6. Now press TIME/SLICES +/- buttons to set the cooking time to 30 minutes.
7. Press "START/STOP" button to start.
8. When the unit beeps to show that it is preheated, open the lid.
9. Arrange the pan over the wire rack and insert in the oven.
10. After 25 minutes of cooking, stir the wine into mushroom mixture.
11. When cooking time is completed, open the lid and serve hot.

Chapter 8

Dessert Recipes

Scalloped Pineapple

Prep time: 5 minutes | Cook time: 30 minutes |Serves 6

- 3 eggs, lightly beaten
- 1/2 cup butter, melted
- 8 oz can pineapple, crushed
- 11/2 cups sugar
- 1/2 cup brown sugar
- 4 cups of bread cubes
- 1/4 cup milk

1. In a large bowl, combine together eggs, milk, butter, brown sugar, pineapple, and sugar.
2. Add bread cubes and stir until well coated.
3. Pour mixture into the greased baking dish.
4. Select bake mode then set the temperature to 350°F and time for 30 minutes. Press start.
5. Once the oven is preheated then place the baking dish into the oven.
6. Serve and enjoy.

Choco Chip Bars

Prep time: 5 minutes | Cook time: 30 minutes |Serves 12

- 2 eggs, lightly beaten
- 11/2 cups chocolate chips
- 1/2 tsp baking soda
- 11/2 cup all-purpose flour
- 1 tsp vanilla
- 1/2 cup sugar
- 1/2 cup brown sugar
- 1 stick butter

1. In a large bowl, beat butter with sugar, vanilla, and brown sugar until fluffy.
2. Add eggs and vanilla and beat well.
3. Mix together flour and baking soda and add into the egg mixture and mix until just combined. Add 1 cup chocolate chips and fold well.
4. Pour batter into the greased baking dish. Sprinkle remaining chocolate chips on top.
5. Select bake mode then set the temperature to 350°F and time for 30 minutes. Press start.
6. Once the oven is preheated then place the baking dish into the oven.
7. Slice and serve.

Bourbon Vanilla Bread Pudding

Prep time: 10 minutes | Cook time: 20 minutes | Serves 4

- 3 slices whole grain bread, cubed
- 1 large egg
- 1 cup whole milk
- 2 tbsp bourbon
- ½ tsp vanilla extract
- ¼ cup maple syrup, divided
- ½ tsp ground cinnamon
- 2 tsp sparkling sugar

1. Select the BAKE function and preheat AIR FRYER OVEN to 270°F.
2. Spray a baking pan with nonstick cooking spray, then place the bread cubes in the pan.
3. In a medium bowl, whisk together the egg, milk, bourbon, vanilla extract, 3 tbsp of maple syrup, and cinnamon. Pour the egg mixture over the bread and press down with a spatula to coat all the bread, then sprinkle the sparkling sugar on top and bake for 20 minutes.
4. Remove the pudding from the air fryer oven and allow to cool in the pan on a wire rack for 10 minutes. Drizzle the remaining 1 tbsp of maple syrup on top. Slice and serve warm.

Roasted Cashews

Prep time: 5 minutes | Cook time: 5 minutes | Serves 6

- 1½ cups raw cashew nuts
- 1 tsp butter, melted
- salt and freshly ground black pepper, as required

1. In a bowl, mix all the ingredients together.
2. Press "Power" button of Air Fry Oven and turn the dial to select "Air Fry" mode.
3. Press TIME/SLICE button and again turn the dial to set the cooking time to 5 minutes.
4. Now push TEMP/DARKNESS button and rotate the dial to set the temperature at 355 °F.
5. Press "Start/Pause" button to start.
6. When the unit beeps to show that it is preheated, open the oven door.
7. Arrange the cashews into the air fry basket and insert in the oven.
8. Shake the cashews once halfway through.
9. When cooking time is completed, open the oven door and transfer the cashews into a heatproof bowl.
10. Serve warm.

Roasted Honey Pears

Prep time: 5 minutes | Cook time: 20 minutes | Serves 4

- 2 large Bosc pears, halved and deseeded
- 3 tbsp honey
- 1 tbsp unsalted butter
- ½ tsp ground cinnamon
- ¼ cup walnuts, chopped
- ¼ cup part skim low-fat ricotta cheese, divided

1. Select the ROAST function and preheat AIR FRYER OVEN to 350°F.
2. In a baking pan, place the pears, cut side up.
3. In a small microwave-safe bowl, melt the honey, butter, and cinnamon. Brush this mixture over the cut sides of the pears.
4. Pour 3 tbsp of water around the pears in the pan. Roast the pears for 20 minutes, or until tender when pierced with a fork and slightly crisp on the edges, basting once with the liquid in the pan.
5. Carefully remove the pears from the pan and place on a serving plate. Drizzle each with some liquid from the pan, sprinkle the walnuts on top, and serve with a spoonful of ricotta cheese.

Banana and Nuts Cake

Prep time: 10 minutes | Cook time: 25 minutes | Serves 6

- 1 pound bananas, mashed
- 8 oz. flour
- 6 oz. sugar
- 3.5 oz. walnuts, chopped
- 2.5 oz. butter, melted
- 2 eggs, lightly beaten
- ¼ tsp baking soda

1. Select the BAKE function and preheat AIR FRYER OVEN to 355°F.
2. In a bowl, combine the sugar, butter, egg, flour, and baking soda with a whisk. Stir in the bananas and walnuts.
3. Transfer the mixture to a greased baking dish. Put the dish in the air fryer oven and bake for 10 minutes.
4. Reduce the temperature to 330°F and bake for another 15 minutes. Serve hot.

Creamy Lime Mousse

Prep time: 5 minutes | Cook time: 12 minutes |Serves 2

- 4 Poz. cream cheese, softened
- ½ cup heavy cream
- 2 tbsp fresh lime juice
- 2 tbsp maple syrup
- A Pinch of salt
- 2 tbsp heavy whipping cream

1. In a bowl, add all the ingredients and mix until well combined.
2. Transfer the mixture into 2 ramekins.
3. Select "BAKE" mode and the cooking time to 12 minutes.
4. Set the temperature at 350 °F.
5. Press the "START/PAUSE" button to start.
6. Arrange the ramekins over the wire rack and insert them in the oven. When the unit beeps to show that cooking time is completed, press the "Power" button to stop cooking and open the door.
7. Remove from oven and set the ramekins aside to cool.
8. Refrigerate the ramekins for at least 3 hours before serving.

Peanut Brittle Bars

Prep Time: 15 minutes|Cook Time: 28 minutes|- Serves 6

- 1 ½ cups all-purpose flour
- ½ cup whole wheat flour
- 1 cup packed brown sugar
- 1 tsp baking soda
- ¼ tsp salt
- 1 cup butter
- 1 cup milk chocolate chips
- 2 cups salted peanuts
- 12 ¼ oz. caramel ice cream topping
- 3 tbsp all-purpose flour

1. Mix flours with salt, baking soda, and brown sugar in a large bowl.
2. Spread the batter in a greased sheet pan.
3. Transfer the pan to the 2nd rack position of Air fryer oven and close the door.
4. Select the "Air Fry" Mode using FUNCTION +/- buttons and select Rack Level 2.
5. Set its cooking time to 12 minutes and temperature to 350 °F, then press "START/STOP" to initiate cooking.
6. Spread chocolate chips and peanuts on top.
7. Mix flour with caramels topping in a bowl and spread on top,
8. Bake again for 16 minutes.
9. Serve.

Chapter 9

Dehydrated and Rotisserie Recipes

Mushroom Slices

Prep time: 5 minutes | Cook time: 5 hours |Serves 4

- 1 cup mushrooms, clean & cut into 1/8-inch thick slices
- 1/4 tbsp fresh lemon juice
- Salt

1. Add sliced mushrooms, lemon juice, and salt into the bowl and toss well.
2. Arrange mushroom slices in an air fryer basket and place the basket in the oven.
3. Select dehydrate then set the temperature to 160°F and time to 5 hours. Press start.
4. Store in a container.

Nutritious Almonds

Prep time: 5 minutes | Cook time: 12 hours |Serves 4

- 1 cup almonds, soaked in water for overnight
- 1/4 tsp cayenne
- 1/2 tbsp olive oil

1. Toss almonds with oil and cayenne.
2. Spread almonds in an air fryer basket and place the basket in the oven.
3. Select dehydrate then set the temperature to 125°F and time to 12 hours. Press start.
4. Store in a container.

Dried Pineapple Pieces

Prep time: 5 minutes | Cook time: 12 hours |Serves 2

- 1 cup pineapple chunks

1. Arrange pineapple chunks in an air fryer basket and place the basket in the oven.
2. Select dehydrate then set the temperature to 135 °F and time to 12 hours. Press start.
3. Store in an air-tight container.

Pork Jerky

Prep time: 5 minutes | Cook time: 5 hours |Serves 4

- 1 lb pork lean meat, sliced thinly
- 1 tsp chili powder
- 1 tsp smoked paprika
- 1/2 tsp garlic powder
- Pepper
- Salt

1. Add paprika, garlic powder, chili powder, pepper, and salt in a bowl and mix well.
2. Add the sliced meat and mix well.
3. Cover and place in the refrigerator overnight.
4. Arrange meat slices in an air fryer basket and place the basket in the oven.
5. Select dehydrate then set the temperature to 160 °F and time to 5 hours. Press start.
6. Store in a container.

Apple and Vegetable Stuffed Turkey

Prep time: 30 minutes | Cook time: 3 hours | Serves 12 to 14

- 1 (12-pound/5.4-kg) turkey, giblet removed, rinsed and pat dry

For the Seasoning:
- ¼ cup lemon pepper
- 2 tbsp chopped fresh parsley
- 1 tbsp celery salt
- 2 cloves garlic, minced
- 2 tsp ground black pepper
- 1 tsp sage

For the Stuffing:
- 1 medium onion, cut into 8 equal parts
- 1 carrot, sliced
- 1 apple, cored and cut into 8 thick slices

1. Mix together the seasoning in a small bowl. Rub over the surface and inside of the turkey.
2. Stuff the turkey with the onions, carrots, and apples. Using the rotisserie spit, push through the turkey and attach the rotisserie forks.
3. If desired, place aluminum foil onto the drip pan. (It makes for easier clean-up!)
4. Select the ROAST function and preheat AIR FRYER OVEN to 350°F. Press ROTATE button and set time to 3 hours.
5. Once preheated, place the prepared turkey with rotisserie spit into the oven.
6. When cooking is complete, the internal temperature should read at least 180°F. Remove the lamb leg using the rotisserie handle and, using hot pads or gloves, carefully remove the turkey from the spit.
7. Server hot.

Strawberry Slices

**Prep time: 5 minutes | Cook time: 12 hours
|Serves 3**

- 1 cup strawberries, cut into 1/8-inch thick slices

1. Arrange strawberry slices in an air fryer basket and place the basket in the oven.
2. Select dehydrate then set the temperature to 130 °F and time to 12 hours. Press start.
3. Store in a container.

Zucchini Chips

**Prep time: 5 minutes | Cook time: 10 hours
|Serves 4**

- 4 cups zucchini slices
- 3 tbsp BBQ sauce

1. Add zucchini slices into the bowl. Pour BBQ sauce over zucchini slices and mix well.
2. Arrange zucchini slices in an air fryer basket and place the basket in the oven.
3. Select dehydrate then set the temperature to 135 °F and time to 10 hours. Press start.
4. Store in a container.

Prime Rib Roast with Mustard Rub

Prep time: 10 minutes | Cook time: 2 hours | Serves 8 to 10

- 1 4-bone prime rib roast (8 to 10 pounds)

Rub:

- ½ cup grainy mustard
- ¼ cup olive oil
- 1 large shallot, finely chopped
- 3 tbsp kosher salt
- 1½ tbsp chopped fresh marjoram
- 1 tbsp chopped fresh thyme
- 1 tbsp coarsely ground black pepper

1. Trim off any straggling pieces of meat or fat from the roast. If the fat cap is too thick, cut it down to between ¼ to ½ inch in thickness depending on how you like your prime rib.
2. To make the rub: Combine the rub ingredients in a small bowl and coat the roast thoroughly with it. Loosely cover with plastic wrap and let the roast sit at room temperature for 30 minutes.
3. Run a long sword skewer through the center of the roast lengthwise to create a pilot hole. Run the rotisserie spit through the hole and secure with the forks. Balance as necessary.
4. Select the ROAST function and preheat AIR FRYER OVEN to 400°F. Press ROTATE button and set time to 2 hours.
5. Place the roast on the preheated air fryer oven, set a drip pan underneath, and add 1 to 2 cups hot water to the pan. Add more water to the pan as necessary.
6. Roast until it is near the desired doneness: 125°F for rare, 135°F for medium rare, 145°F for medium, 155°F for medium well, or 165°F for well done. The roast will shrink during cooking, so adjust the forks when appropriate. Remove the roast when it is 5°F to 10°F below the desired doneness. It will continue to cook during the resting phase.
7. Carefully remove the rotisserie forks and slide the spit out, and then place the roast on a large cutting board. Tent the roast with aluminum foil and a kitchen towel and let the meat rest for 15 to 20 minutes. Cut away the bones first by passing a knife against the bones and cutting through (save the bones for later). Cut the meat into thin slices.

Appendix 1 Measurement Conversion Chart

Volume Equivalents (Dry)

US STANDARD	METRIC (APPROXIMATE)
1/8 teaspoon	0.5 mL
1/4 teaspoon	1 mL
1/2 teaspoon	2 mL
3/4 teaspoon	4 mL
1 teaspoon	5 mL
1 tablespoon	15 mL
1/4 cup	59 mL
1/2 cup	118 mL
3/4 cup	177 mL
1 cup	235 mL
2 cups	475 mL
3 cups	700 mL
4 cups	1 L

Weight Equivalents

US STANDARD	METRIC (APPROXIMATE)
1 ounce	28 g
2 ounces	57 g
5 ounces	142 g
10 ounces	284 g
15 ounces	425 g
16 ounces (1 pound)	455 g
1.5 pounds	680 g
2 pounds	907 g

Volume Equivalents (Liquid)

US STANDARD	US STANDARD (OUNCES)	METRIC (APPROXIMATE)
2 tablespoons	1 fl.oz.	30 mL
1/4 cup	2 fl.oz.	60 mL
1/2 cup	4 fl.oz.	120 mL
1 cup	8 fl.oz.	240 mL
1 1/2 cup	12 fl.oz.	355 mL
2 cups or 1 pint	16 fl.oz.	475 mL
4 cups or 1 quart	32 fl.oz.	1 L
1 gallon	128 fl.oz.	4 L

Temperatures Equivalents

FAHRENHEIT(F)	CELSIUS(C) APPROXIMATE
225 °F	107 °C
250 °F	120 ° °C
275 °F	135 °C
300 °F	150 °C
325 °F	160 °C
350 °F	180 °C
375 °F	190 °C
400 °F	205 °C
425 °F	220 °C
450 °F	235 °C
475 °F	245 °C
500 °F	260 °C

Appendix 2 The Dirty Dozen and Clean Fifteen

The Environmental Working Group (EWG) is a nonprofit, nonpartisan organization dedicated to protecting human health and the environment Its mission is to empower people to live healthier lives in a healthier environment. This organization publishes an annual list of the twelve kinds of produce, in sequence, that have the highest amount of pesticide residue-the Dirty Dozen-as well as a list of the fifteen kinds ofproduce that have the least amount of pesticide residue-the Clean Fifteen.

THE DIRTY DOZEN

The 2016 Dirty Dozen includes the following produce. These are considered among the year's most important produce to buy organic:

Strawberries	Spinach
Apples	Tomatoes
Nectarines	Bell peppers
Peaches	Cherry tomatoes
Celery	Cucumbers
Grapes	Kale/collard greens
Cherries	Hot peppers

The Dirty Dozen list contains two additional itemskale/collard greens and hot peppers-because they tend to contain trace levels of highly hazardous pesticides.

THE CLEAN FIFTEEN

The least critical to buy organically are the Clean Fifteen list. The following are on the 2016 list:

Avocados	Papayas
Corn	Kiw
Pineapples	Eggplant
Cabbage	Honeydew
Sweet peas	Grapefruit
Onions	Cantaloupe
Asparagus	Cauliflower
Mangos	

Some of the sweet corn sold in the United States are made from genetically engineered (GE) seedstock. Buy organic varieties of these crops to avoid GE produce.

Appendix 3 Index

A

almond 10, 27
apple 41, 59
asparagus 48
avocado 19, 36

B

bacon 13, 42
balsamic vinegar 48
basil 27, 41
BBQ sauce 60
bell pepper 26, 29
bread 13, 15, 20, 22, 23, 27, 28, 44, 52, 53
broccoli 17
butter 10, 12, 14, 15, 28, 29, 36, 38, 41, 44, 46, 47, 49, 50

C

cauliflower 9
cayenne 33, 57
cayenne pepper 33
Cheddar cheese 9, 21
cheese 9, 11, 13, 14, 17, 18, 21, 23, 25, 26, 27, 39, 47
chicken 25, 26, 27, 28, 29, 30, 31, 35, 41
chili powder 13, 36, 58
chives 41
cinnamon 10, 12, 15, 33, 53, 54
coconut 10, 18
corn 43
cumin 13, 33, 36

D

Dijon mustard 38, 42

E

egg 9, 11, 13, 15, 17, 19, 20, 21, 22, 23, 27, 28, 36, 43, 49, 52, 53

F

fresh chives 41
fresh parsley 21, 32, 59
fresh thyme 28, 34, 46, 52
fish fillets 43

G

garlic 9, 18, 25, 26, 28, 31, 33, 35, 37, 38, 39, 41, 44
garlic powder 9, 18, 25, 28, 38, 50, 58

H

honey 12, 47, 48, 54
heavy cream 55

I

Italian seasoning 23

J

juice 26, 27, 30, 31, 35, 38, 41, 43, 55, 57

K

kosher salt 14, 15, 38, 61

L

lemon 26, 27, 30, 31, 35, 38, 41, 44, 57, 59
lemon juice 26, 27, 30, 31, 35, 38, 41, 57
lime 43, 46, 55
lime juice 43, 55

.M

maple syrup 10, 15, 53, 55
marinara sauce 18
milk 9, 10, 12, 14, 15, 52, 53, 55
Mozzarella 39
mushrooms 46, 48, 50, 57
mustard 27, 38, 42, 44, 61
mixed bell peppers 24, 43, 52

N

nuts 53

O

olive oil 11, 25, 31, 34, 35, 38, 39, 42, 43, 47, 48, 57, 61
onion 13, 17, 23, 26, 28, 29, 31, 33, 34, 35, 36, 37, 44, 46, 59
onion powder 23
oregano 26, 35

P

paprika 26, 27, 58
potato 25
pineapple chunks 58
parmesan cheese 48
panko breadcrumbs 19

R

raisins 10
rosemary 30, 31, 34, 35, 37, 38, 39, 49
ricotta cheese 54

S

salt 9, 10, 11, 12, 13, 14, 15, 18, 19, 23, 25, 27, 31, 34, 35
soy sauce 28, 37, 48
strawberries 60
syrup 10, 15, 53, 55
sugar 28, 42, 54

T

tomato 13
turmeric 13

U

unsalted butter 15, 28, 54

W

white wine 50
walnut 54
Worcestershire sauce 38

Y

yogurt 32, 38, 42

Z

zucchini slices 60

Hey there!

Wow, can you believe we've reached the end of this culinary journey together? I'm truly thrilled and filled with joy as I think back on all the recipes we've shared and the flavors we've discovered. This experience, blending a bit of tradition with our own unique twists, has been a journey of love for good food. and knowing you've been out there, giving these dishes a try, has made this adventure incredibly special to me.

Even though we're turning the last page of this book, I hope our conversation about all things delicious doesn't have to end. I cherish your thoughts, your experiments, and yes, even those moments when things didn't go as planned. Every piece of feedback you share is invaluable, helping to enrich this experience for us all.

I'd be so grateful if you could take a moment to share your thoughts with me, be it through a review on Amazon or any other place you feel comfortable expressing yourself online. Whether it's praise, constructive criticism, or even an idea for how we might do things differently in the future, your input is what truly makes this journey meaningful.

This book is a piece of my heart, offered to you with all the love and enthusiasm I have for cooking. But it's your engagement and your words that elevate it to something truly extraordinary.

Thank you from the bottom of my heart for being such an integral part of this culinary adventure. Your openness to trying new things and sharing your experiences has been the greatest gift.

Catch you later,

Wendy C. Thomas

Made in United States
Cleveland, OH
01 December 2024

10913039R00042